W9-BYB-792

DISCARDED
From Nashville Public Library

Property of
The Public Library of Nashville and Davidson County
225 Polk Ave., Nashville, TN 37203

AMAZING STRING TRICKS

Written by
Kirk Charles

Illustrated by
Viki Woodworth

Text copyright © 1996 by The Child's World, Inc.
All rights reserved. No part of this book may be
reproduced or utilized in any form or by any means
without written permission from the Publisher.
Printed in the United States of America.

Library of Congress Catalog-in-Publication Data
Charles, Kirk.
Amazing string tricks / by Kirk Charles; illustrated by Viki Woodworth.
p. cm.
Summary: Provides instructions for a variety of string tricks.
ISBN 1-56766-085-1
1. Tricks--Juvenile literature. 2. String--Juvenile literature.
[1. Magic tricks.]
I. Woodworth, Viki, ill.   II. Title.
GV1559.C44 1996   93-35866
793.8--dc20   CIP/AC

For magic tricks to be wonderful and mysterious, there are certain rules you must follow:

1. Never reveal the secrets of the magic. To do so ruins the magic and spoils the fun.

2. Never tell the audience what you are going to do before you do it. Surprise is very important to making good magic.

3. Never repeat the trick for the same audience during the same show. They will know what's going to happen and will probably figure out the trick.

4. Stories make the magic more mysterious. So make up a story that will go with your trick.

5. Practice each trick many times before you show it to anyone. Without practicing, you might accidentally reveal the secret.

Make a trick bird feeder. Tie an unsalted peanut in its shell to a long piece of string and hang it in a tree. Many birds love peanuts.

Equal Strings

This is a very fair trick, all things being equal!

   What happens: A short piece of string and a long piece of string magically become the same size.

   What you need: A short piece of string and a long piece of string.

1. Before you begin the show, loop the small piece of string around the long piece, about four inches from one end.

2. Hide the spot where the two strings come together between your thumb and finger. The two ends of small piece will be sticking up out of your hand. The two ends of the long piece will be hanging down out of your hand. This looks like two unequal pieces of string side by side.

3. Bring the longest hanging end of the string up to the other hanging end, until the two are side by side.

4. Pull on the two hanging ends and they will seem to change in size.

5. Show that the two strings are now about the same length.

Then put the string away, because you don't want anyone to examine it.

hide loop under thumb and finger

Invisible Knot

This is the Invisible Man's favorite trick!

What happens: A knot appears on a length of string.

What you need: A piece of string about twelve inches long and a secret knot.

1. Before you show the string, secretly tie a knot about two inches from one end.

2. Hold the string in your right fist, hiding the knot under your curled fingers. Leave the end near the knot sticking up out of your hand.

3. Ask the audience if they would like to see the invisible knot.

4. After they say, "Yes," point to a spot on the other end of the string. Say, "There it is. You can't see it, because it's invisible." Tell them you'll make the knot visible.

5. Grab the lower end of the string with your left fingers and bring it up to your right hand. Place the lower end between your right first finger and thumb.

6. Swing your right hand back and forth, and then open your finger and thumb so the end falls down. No knot appears! Act surprised and try it again.

7. Repeat steps 5 and 6.

8. Repeat step 5 again (but not step 6).

9. Swing your right hand back and forth, but this time open your other fingers, instead of your first finger and thumb. The other end of the string - the end with the knot - will fall, so the knot will be visible. Hand the string to someone and let them untie it.

hide
knot in
hand →

Fastest Knot in the West

This is not a trick, but rather a way of showing
off your new skills.

    What happens: You quickly tie a knot in
a string.

    What you need: A piece of string about two feet
long and some patience.

For this to work, you must hold the string in a special way. Make sure you hold it as the illustration shows.

1. Hold one end of the string in the crotch of your left thumb. The end should stick up above your hand.

2. Pass the other end of the string over the back of your right hand. Drape it loosely over your right first finger, near the thumb. Use your thumb to hold it against your finger. Let the end hang down below your right hand.

3. Bring your hands together, with the fingertips pointing toward each other.

4. With the first and second fingers of each hand, pinch the end of the string held in the opposite hand.

5. Open both thumbs.

6. Draw your hands apart and the knot automatically appears.

Disappearing Knot

This knot is sometimes called a slip knot - but it's not really a knot at all.

What happens: You tie a knot and then make it disappear.

What you need: A piece of string about two feet long.

Make sure you follow the illustration.

1. In the middle of the string, make a loop by twisting the right section over the left. The loop should point down.

2. Reach your right hand through the loop. Grab the right-hand section of the string between your right thumb and first finger and form another loop without twisting it. Bring this new loop back through the first loop.

3. At the same time, relax your left thumb so that the right-hand section it was holding against your finger is free.

4. Pull with your right finger and thumb until the string tightens around the loop.

5. Let go of the string with your right hand.

6. With your right hand, grab the right end of the string and pull on it. The slip knot will tighten and then seem to disappear.

The Sliding Knot

This is a classic trick used by many magicians.

What happens: A knot tied on a string moves.

What you need: A long piece of string and a short piece of string.

1. Before the show begins, tie the short piece of string around the long piece. When you are done it will look like two equal pieces of string are tied together.

2. Show the string and say that you will try to do an amazing trick.

3. Grab the knot and move it slowly down the string until it comes off.

tie small piece of string
on long piece

The Pop-Off Knot

Clowns like to use this trick, because it's surprising and looks funny.

  What happens: A knot tied on a piece of string pops off when you pull the string.

  What you need: A short piece of string and a long piece of string.

1. Before the show begins, make a loop with the small piece and hide it in your left closed fist. Make sure all the ends of the small piece point down.

2. Show the long piece of string to your audience, holding it in your right hand.

3. With both hands, make a loop in the middle of the long piece of string.

4. With your right hand take the string by the loop, and place it into your left closed fist, entering your fist near the little finger. Your right hand releases the string.

5. Hold both pieces of string with your left hand.

6. Insert your right first finger and thumb into your left fist, near the thumb.

7. With your right first finger and thumb, pull up the small looped piece of string, which looks like the middle loop of the long string.

8. Cut this loop into two parts.

9. Cut this loop several more times, until it is cut away.

10. Put the scissors down. Make a magical pass over your left hand then show that the string is together again.

hide small loop in palm

19

The Escape

This is a trick Harry Houdini would have liked.

What happens: Two rings magically penetrate string.

What you need: Two rings, one pencil, and two long pieces of string the same size.

1. Drape one piece of string over one end of the pencil. Then drape the other piece of string over the other end of the pencil.

2. Have someone hold the pencil so you can adjust the two strings. Center each string on the pencil, so that the ends hang evenly.

3. Tie the two strings together tightly. They will be tied around the pencil.

4. Thread one ring onto one pair of string strands. Thread the other ring onto the other pair of string strands.

5. Have someone hold one pair of strands in each hand.

6. Take one strand from each of your assistant's hands and tie them together over the rings.

7. Give the strand that is now on your right side to the assistant's right hand. Give the strand that is now on your left side to the assistant's left hand.

8. Explain how you have tied the string around the pencil and the rings. Say that it would be impossible for the rings to escape.

9. Slide the pencil out of the strings.

10. Have your assistant pull on the strings, and the rings will fall off.

tie middle two together

The Rising Tube Illusion

Here's a trick you can build.

What happens: A cardboard tube seems to rise and fall mysteriously.

What you need: A cardboard tube, a piece of string twice as long as the tube, a shorter piece of string the same size as the tube, some tape, and a paper clip.

Before the show, you need to build the equipment.

1. Put the shorter piece of string into the tube.

2. Tape the string to the inside of the tube near the end.

3. Tie the longer string to the paper clip.

4. Hold the tube so the taped string comes out the lower end.

5. Lower the longer string tied to the paper clip down into the tube.

6. Keep lowering the longer string until the paper clip comes out the lower end of the tube.

7. Thread the short taped string through the clip.

8. Hold on to the shorter string. Pull up on the longer string until the clip disappears back into the tube. It looks like one piece of string goes through the tube. You are now ready to show the trick.

9. Hold the tube so it stands up in your right hand.

10. Pinch the shorter string, near its end, between your right first and second fingers.

11. Pull up on the longer string and the tube will rise.

12. Lower the longer string and the tube will drop.

tape

thread small string through paper clip

tie long string onto paper clip

This Book Is About Magic Tricks Using String.

It is written by a real magician, Kirk Charles. Kirk has performed thousands of magic shows, some for children and some for grown-ups. He has done magic for television shows, commercials, and movies. He has also written magic books for magicians.

Kirk wants you to know that he did not invent these tricks. They came from many different sources. Kirk learned some from books and some from other magicians.

The way to learn the tricks is to do them! So make sure you have all the items you need as you read the tricks.

Kirk hopes that you will learn some of these tricks and practice them before you do them. People of all ages love good magic, and the way to perform good magic is to practice!

Read all the instructions for each trick before trying it. If you read something you don't understand, ask your mom, your dad, your older brother, or your older sister to help. But ask them to keep the trick secret.